How To Transition From Employee To Business Owner

With Action Steps

By

Boomy Tokan

Copyright © Boomy Tokan 2013

All rights reserved. No part of this publication may be reproduced in any form, electronic or mechanical, including scanning, photocopying or any information storage or retrieval system without the prior written permission of the copyright holder.

Disclaimer

License Terms

This course is for your own personal use ONLY. It is STRICTLY PROHIBITED to reproduce the content enclosed herein or to distribute this course to any third party, or via any third party website. All content is protected by Copyright ©.

Income Disclaimer

This document contains business strategies, marketing methods and other business advice that, regardless of my own results and experience, may not produce the same results (or any results) for you.

I make absolutely no guarantee, expressed or implied that by following the advice below you will make any money or improve current profits, as there are several factors and variables that come into play regarding any given business.

Primarily, results will depend on the nature of the product or business model, the conditions of the marketplace, the experience of the individual, the application of said principles, and situations and elements that are beyond your control.

As with any business endeavor, you assume all risk related to investment and money based on your own discretion and at your own potential expense.

Liability Disclaimer

By reading this document, you assume all risks associated with using the advice given below, with the full understanding that you, solely, are responsible for anything that may occur as a result of putting this information into action in any way, and regardless of your interpretation of the advice.

You further agree that the author cannot be held responsible in any way for the success or failure of your business as a result of the information presented below.

It is your responsibility to conduct your own due diligence regarding the safe and successful operation of your business if you intend to apply any of this information in any way to your business operations.

COPYRIGHT © 2014 Boomy Tokan - ALL RIGHTS RESERVED.

FREE Bonus

How To Start Your Own Business In 30 Days"

Hey ... If you would like to learn how to start and run a "High Performance" business; then download this FREE guide. It will also show you how to start making money from your business within 30 Days!

"How To Start Your Own Business In 30 Days"

Copy and paste in your browser:
www.startyourownbusinessacademy.com/freedownload1

Enjoy

Content

Disclaimer

FREE Bonus

Introduction

The Important First Step - Don't Major On The Minor

Chapter 1-Test yourself, to see if you are ready to start your own business

    Be aware of the hurdles to jump!

    Make a roadmap today!

    Test your skills

    Conclusion

Chapter 2: Be Mentally and Psychologically - Solidifying your dreams with concrete plans and actions

    Understanding what it takes to run a business is the key to its success.

    Helpful Tips!

    Conclusion

Chapter 3: Learn to do your current job better

    Reasons why you need to do your current Job Better!

How to do your Job better

Conclusions

Chapter 4: You Cannot Have Your Cake and Eat It (at least for a while)!

Change your lifestyle

Conclusion

Chapter 5: Time – This is the "Achilles Heel" for most people

To leave your comfort zone!

Solutions

Conclusion

Chapter 6: Cut Down Your Expenses

How to save money for your business?

Conclusion

Chapter 7: Work Part Time or Start Your Business Part Time

Pros and Cons of starting a Part Time Business

Tips for Making your Decision

Conclusion

Chapter 8: Role of the Family in Your Business Start-up

How to move your family along a paradigm shift

1. Communication

2. Convince your Friends & Relatives

3. Maintain a healthy Work-life balance

4. Sell them the dreams

5. Don't share business problems at the dinner table unless your family probe for it!

6. Get them involved in doing some of the research

7. Celebrate the milestones

Conclusion

Chapter 9: The Business Plan

The Five Parts of a Business Plan

Think about your hand. It has five fingers, right (hopefully)? Or just imagine you have five fingers. In the same way I want you to know that there are five parts to a business plan:

What Each Title Stands for:

Other components to consider:

Define Your Target Market

Position Your Business

Pricing

    Identify and Analyse Your Competition

    Conclusion.

Chapter 10: Go Cold Turkey

    Conclusion

Final Chapter

FREE Bonus

Other Books by Boomy Tokan

"How To Write Your First Business Plan"

Introduction & Chapter 1

Book Title: Business Funding Secrets:

Read Introduction & Chapter 1

"70 Public Speaking Tips"

Read Introduction & Chapter 1

The Bad Girls Of The Bible

Read Introduction & Chapter 1

Profile

Introduction

Every year, millions of people around the world start businesses, and by experience, a high proportion of those Start-ups are created by those currently employed.

Since there are no longer jobs for life, many are opting to take charge of their own future by setting up businesses they can drive and control. Also, the internet offers many opportunities such as; the ability to work from home while raising a family, convenience, efficiency, closeness with sellers/buyers, and the intrinsic value of being able to create a better working life balance.

All in all, we see more people taking on the mantle of starting their own businesses!

However, along with this good news comes the challenge of being able to create a business that grows and avoids the statistics of becoming one of the many failed ventures.

Therefore, it is important to adequately understand what will be involved in running a business, and how to navigate around pitfalls.

This book has been written as a practical approach to help those in employment who are considering starting a business, along with the personal challenges they need to overcome and how to create a route to success.

My goal is that as you read through the content, it will spark the desire to build with the right foundation, so that the storms of life will not erode your dream of owning and running a successful enterprise!

Enjoy!
Boomy Tokan

The Important First Step - Don't Major On The Minor

I remember a video I watched on YouTube about starting a business. In those 3 minutes, the officious looking presenter explained that if you want to start a business, the first 3 things to do were to:
- Establish a limited liability company/LLC or a Sole Proprietorship
- Get a domain name
- Develop a business plan

As good as the above sounds, it is actually a time wasting and 'Money in the bin' approach to starting a business. I did not realise until the end of the video that the presenter was actually an accountant who was selling his services!

Sadly, that is how most people (especially some of those in employment) think about starting in business: "They Major on the

Minor". They focus on some of the most irrelevant factors, and end up spending (wasting) money, before they even leave the starting block. I guess they still think of the "Old School" way of starting a business. The problem becomes more acute if those individuals have money they can throw at a venture at the initial stages.

Why is the above approach ridiculous?

If you set up a limited liability company/or an LLC even before you have tested your product, what makes you think that it is the best approach? Besides, once you have registered a business structure, you need to comply with the required laws, which take time and money! Some even get hung up on getting business cards and logos before they sell a single thing. People spend thousands creating the best looking logos for an idea that will never take off.

Why buy a domain name before you know your target group? The target group should dictate the keywords, and you cannot determine a target group until you have figured out the problems you want to solve and how you plan to do it. Your initial focus should not be creating a fancy website even before you know what to sell (except you are using this site to generate useful information).

Somebody says: "Isn't that all part of the preparation process?" My answer is that it could be if you are at the stage that requires such an expense. So what do you need to do? What steps do you need to take?

Let me give you the new approach that I hope you will follow:
- Write down your dream & skills – It will cost you nothing to get a sheet of paper or your computer to write out in as much detail as possible what you want to achieve and the skills you have.

- Then write out the problems - you want to solve for the growing niche you have identified.
- Testing – Once you have written this out as clearly as possible, you then need to come up with a cheap and cheerful way to test your idea/determine its viability
- Free Tools – the best way to test is by using online methods and thank GOD there are so many free tools. You don't need to develop a fancy website, instead set up a free Facebook page or free site from https://www.blogger.com. The good news is that you can have as many pages as you like. This gives you the opportunity to test keywords, phrases and anything else. You don't need to buy an email marketing service, when you can use the free product that MailChimp.com has. With this free product and other apps from companies like Woobox.com, you can set an opt-in

page on your Facebook to collect emails. Use the free service offered by surveymonkey.com too!
- What I am saying is that your ideas change so much at the beginning stages, the last thing you want to do is start spending money before you make any!
- Advertising – some people might even start considering taking out ads in local papers in the early stages of business. Why not use Facebook Ads instead? It is cheaper, much more targeted, and gives immediate response.
- Immediate Response - Here is one reason why you must test your ideas online. Things change so fast that when starting in business, 4 weeks is a long time to realise your ad boomed or that the service was not needed. If you place an ad on Facebook and no one is clicking after 12 hours, you either targeted the wrong audience or your idea needs work.

It's Immediate; It's Now – this allows you to respond.

Once you have done the above and you know your product sells, then it will be easy to know what kind of structure to have, the domain name/s to buy, and the kind of information you need in your business plan.

Some people even think that if they don't buy a domain name or take an advertising opportunity being sold to them immediately, then they miss out forever.

I say you should learn from Richard Branson's quote that says: "Opportunities are like buses; there is always another one coming along."
Besides, the last thing you want to do is to spend all you have, and end up with no resources to run another idea or opportunity.

Don't Put The Cart Before The Horse!

Now that we know this lets move forward!

Chapter 1-Test yourself, to see if you are ready to start your own business

Today people are more worried about their jobs than ever before. Employees face unprecedented challenges in the work place such as the fear of downsizing, company instability and decline in growth, meeting higher targets, increasing time demands etc. Such problems have given rise to the desire for people to become their own boss and direct their own future.

Be aware of the hurdles to jump!

If you are planning such a life changing move, be aware that it is a huge step. If you do not plan well, your whole investment could disappear in a flash.

Below are ten questions that you must answer:
1. Are you ready to quit your job?
2. Are you ready to sacrifice your holidays, family gatherings, social and leisure activities, etc.?
3. Do you have the skills required for business?
4. What will be unique about your business?
5. Have you ample financial resources to start the business?
6. Do you have the required contacts/out sourcing company to assist you?
7. What can you sell or offer to your customers/market niche?
8. How are your products and services different from others?
9. What would be your potential/target population?
10. Do you want to start it, as a full time or a part time business?

Be aware that employment gives you have access to certain perks. You have a fixed salary and allowances (home allowance, travel allowance, personal and family insurance, etc.). But, if you quit your job, you may lose all these perks and privileges.

Also be prepared to work hard initially. It is not uncommon for people to work day and night in order to achieve their personal, family and organizational goals. You must be aware that after you start your business, there may be no weekends off, along with a considerable amount of anxiety and stress involved in sourcing and fulfilling orders.

Make a roadmap today!

One of the most important decisions to make when starting your own business is, whether you want to quit your job completely and start a full time business, or carry on with your job and start a part-time business. The next chapters will shedlight on that topic, however, the major decision is yours.

When answering the above mentioned questions, don't be over optimistic, but be realistic.

Test your skills

Now is a good time for you to test your abilities. There are some specific behaviours and skills associated with entrepreneurship. These behaviours and characteristics include creativity, innovation, leadership ability, problem solving, communication skills, planning and organizing skills and decision making skills. This simple test will help you determine whether or not you have the required skills.

Please answer these questions either 'True' or 'False'.

1) I don't like people (less competent than me) telling me what to do.
2) I have a vision to be my own boss.
3) I am a team player but often play as a captain.
4) I often advise others on how to solve their problems.
5) I like to challenge myself.
6) I usually work well in difficult situations.
7) I look for better ways to do things.
8) My ideas are appreciated by others.
9) I focus on outcomes rather than process.
10) I cannot leave what I can do today for tomorrow.
11) I often come up with different solutions.
12) I can easily decide "what to do" in a tough situation.
13) I feel comfortable talking in a gathering.
14) I have faith in myself and confidence in my abilities.
15) I try to solve problems by myself.

16) I am detail oriented
17) I often help others to solve their problems.
18) My employer, colleagues, friends, and family have trust in me.
19) I can get things done by gathering the required people together.
20) Most of the members of my family run their own business.

If you answered "True" to more than 15 questions, then you are ready to be an entrepreneur. If you answered "True" to less than 15, but more than 10 questions, then you need to polish your skills. If you have less than 10 "True" answers, you should review your idea to be an entrepreneur by developing your skills.

Conclusion

Starting your own business is not an easy decision. It's a decision that should be considered after careful thought and planning.

You must have requisite skills and resources to start a business, along with the willpower and discipline to sacrifice. If you are willing to develop the necessary aptitudes like decision making, leadership ability, problem solving behaviour, team building skills, communication skills and interpersonal skills then you can consider yourself ready to begin the journey to entrepreneurship!

Chapter 2: Be Mentally and Psychologically - Solidifying your dreams with concrete plans and actions

Most people dream about being in business and would love success to jump on them one day without paying the price! Yet success in business requires patience and hard work. You must prepare yourself before getting into it. Be absolutely persuaded that you want to have your own business, whether that is a "Life Style" enterprise that will generate $100,000 a year or a "Corporation" with a turnover of $100m a year.

Understanding what it takes to run a business is the key to its success.

In Japan, about 70 to 80 percent of businesses are small to medium enterprises, owned by individuals or families. According to the

Deming (Japanese quality guru), when you start any project, spend 90% of the total time in planning. Perhaps this is the reason why Japanese enterprises run by the private owners are so successful and continue to thrive in difficult times! Get involved in your business planning process and spend your leisure time pondering about it. You must think about the novel ideas of doing business, market competition, product competitiveness, cost, etc. Don't put it off for a later or better time – start planning for it today.

Helpful Tips!

So, here are some helpful but important tips to help you solidify your dreams with plans and actions:

    1. Set 'SMART' goals

        Prepare a dossier and record of everything about your business. It would be like a logbook for your business, which would give you the guidelines of what you want and where you are. Set "SMART' goals for your business. SMART is an acronym:

- S for Specific
- M for Measureable
- A for Attainable
- R for Realistic
- T for Timed

Don't be vague while setting your goals; be specific. For example, if you are in a furniture business and you want to set a business goal that after five years, you would be able to sell furniture all over the U.S. You have to set your goal like: "My sales target in year 20_ _ is $10 million." This is a broad goal. Now, subdivide it into different small goals like: in the first quarter, your sales target is $3 million and in the second quarter it is $3.5 million. Your goals must be measureable! You must also keep in mind while setting your goals that they remain achievable. Do consider your resources; like the investments require for achieving this goal or the workforce, marketing budget, etc. Be realistic in your goals; no point thinking your business will turn over 1 million in the first month, when all you can invest is less than $10. Even if it does make that turnover, it will just be a "Spike", "Viral", "Fluke", or whatever title you may give it. Most businesses grow step by step!

2. Read books

Success stories of the entrepreneurs will not only broaden your vision, but boost your confidence. Read books on topics like entrepreneurship, small and medium business management, marketing and finance; it will not only enhance your knowledge but also sharpen your business skills.

3. **Avail networking opportunities**

There are a number of platforms available where you can enhance your vision regarding business. Seminars and conferences on the topic of entrepreneurship can not only provide you with insights about the latest research and development, but can also provide networking opportunities.

4. **Continuously Monitor Your Performance**

When you set certain objectives and targets, stick with it and don't change it without reasonable justification. Monitor your performance continuously by recognizing and fixing the loopholes.

5. Believe in yourself

Initially, you may not fulfil the objectives of your business, but stay focused and believe in yourself and in your abilities. There is no one who can make the situation better except you. Just stick with the plan, and if it deviates somehow, try to resolve the situation with the best available strategy. Always get back on course.

6. Learn from others

You cannot run your business in isolation. Look for an experienced person who can guide you – a Mentor or join a Business Coaching/Mastermind Group. This offers the best opportunity to stay in touch with other business owners; learn from their experiences and avoid reinventing the wheel.

7. Take a part time job in your business field

Investors always look for some form of experience within the industry the budding entrepreneur is attacking. Sometimes the only solution to lack of experience is to get a part-time job or even a voluntary role within the industry you plan to start the business in. It will enhance your strengths; help overcome weaknesses and teach you valuable lessons for your future endeavours.

8. Start taking small steps

There is a famous story of a college girl, who was running a chain of restaurants. She initially started from her college, and then after a few years, she started one restaurant and then a chain of restaurants! If you want to open a book store, purchase a book on discount from a book seller and then sell it to your colleague or friend. Arouse the entrepreneurial spirit in you by taking small steps.

9. Be Prepared for the long haul

You must be clear that running a business it is not a one day or a month affair; it will probably be a lifelong experience. Having a business is not a walk in the park. There are difficult and joyful times ahead. Therefore, prepare your mind and keep on expecting the best.

Conclusion

Success in business requires patience and hard work. You must be psychologically ready before getting into it. Set objectives and goals for yourself and for your business as well. However, the goals should be specific, measureable, achievable, realistic, and time bound. Don't waste your leisure time. Read books and magazines on entrepreneurship, attend seminars, conferences, etc., which will give you the opportunity to network with like minded individuals. Spend time with other business owners, industry professionals and learn from their experiences.

Get yourself completely involved!

Chapter 3: Learn to do your current job better

Most people, who want to start a business, make the mistake of neglecting their current job, even though they cannot afford to do so.

Keep in mind that the loss of attention in your current job could result in being fired. Even if you are thinking of quitting your job for the new business, be aware that it is better to leave with a good recommendation, than being fired.

An important component of your life is your family and children, so don't forget that they will have to suffer if you lose your job unnecessarily.

Therefore, you must stick with your current job and make the most of your position. You can actually leverage your current job experience to sharpen your skills, which would be helpful for the new business. You have to be focused on your key objective (i.e. your potential business) and look for the opportunities you could grab while staying on in the current job.

If you perform well in your current job, you could have a potential client for your own business. Don't forget that you are getting a number of perks from your current employer; if you leave your current job for your business; there is no guarantee that your potential business will be an overnight success.

Your current job is very important for you, therefore, place value on it.

Learn to be more productive, effective and focussed. Experiencing new things will enhance your vision and skills which will benefit your new business as well as your current employer. Don't hesitate to work on new assignments and projects; work whole heartedly. Success in difficult tasks will boost your confidence and bring you closer to your dream business.

This chapter will throw some more light on the reasons why you should perform well on your current job, and will also discuss the major steps that could be followed in order to get the best from your current job.

Reasons why you need to do your current Job Better!

Although, you are planning to start your own business, here are 10 reasons, why you need to do your current job better:

1. Pay checks and other monetary & Non-monetary benefits

Your current job provides you with a continuous stream of earnings plus other benefits like medical insurance, loan facilities, travel expenses, along with a stable financial life. If you perform well in your current job, then you will continue to enjoy these benefits as your business moves towards maturity.

2. A chance for Self-Improvement

Your current job also provides you with several training and development opportunities. After quitting your job and starting your own business, you will be armed with tried and tested strategies that can be implemented. "Do onto others as you want done to you". Work well for someone else so that others will work well for you.

3. Start-ups failure rate

If you quit your job, or your employer sacks you on account of negligence; keep in mind that you are going to start a venture that may not be an instant success.

4. Meet Expectations

Your employer has hired you for a reason and he/she has certain expectations from you. Make sure, you fulfil those expectations and never breach the trust. Always strive to perform above those expectations as you prepare yourself for the future; in this way you become a role model for your own employees!

5. Learn from your Mistakes

Being human, we all make mistakes. Instead of blaming yourself, learn from your mistakes. Your mistakes in the workplace may not be costly for you at this stage, but during your own business, when things have to be managed on your own, mistakes can lead to disasters.

7. Networking Opportunity

Your current job also provides you networking opportunities with your colleagues, customers and suppliers. You can identify the key persons that could be your potential client or suppliers.

8. More Work - A Blessing in Disguise

Don't hesitate to work more if you are planning to start your business. More work will help you to learn and manage priorities which will be beneficial for you as an entrepreneur. So, work hard on your current job and develop this skill.

9. Proactive Approach

Think out of the box and perform your duties in a creative manner. Be proactive and anticipate what will be asked from you. Eagerly offer your services and be a 'can do' person. My advice is that you stay informed about the opportunities that arise in your workplace and react accordingly.

10. Find Solutions to the problems

Don't go to your boss at the first sign of trouble. Instead, try to solve it by yourself. Develop this habit now; it is will stand you in good stead for the future.

How to do your Job better

Hopefully, the above discussion has convinced you that you have to focus on your current job while starting up your new business. You may be concerned about how to manage your business and the job at the same time.

The ideas given below deal with those concerns:

1. Prepare Yourself

You have a dream to be your own boss in the future, so prepare yourself now. Get motivated - knowing that working enthusiastically on your current job is moving you towards your dream not away from it.

2. Prioritise

When you are working and starting a business at the same time you need to be more organised by setting priorities other wise you will become overwhelmed. Everyday write down the top 3 goals you must achieve at work and the top three you must achieve in your business; then make them a reality.
This simple method will ensure you prioritise each day and become more productive.

Another way of thinking about your day is to create a 'to do' list and prioritize your short assignments long term projects, plans for your business, etc. Perform the most important things first, and whenever you are performing any tasks, ask yourself "is this the best use of my time?"

3. Concentrate on the task in hand

Think and concentrate on the task you are currently doing. It will enable you to finish quicker and provide more time to spend on your business.

4. Review your day

Review the activities of your whole day and think about what you achieved. Think about whether or not you have successfully achieved your targets. If not, what were the reasons? More importantly, what will you do differently tomorrow?

Conclusions

During the transition phase from employee to business owner, people mostly neglect their current jobs. Never take your current job as a burden, but as a blessing. You must exert considerable amount of effort in your current job to acquire knowledge, skills, and abilities that will benefit your employer and add value to your future business as well.

See your current job as a stepping stone towards your own business!

Chapter 4: You Cannot Have Your Cake and Eat It (at least for a while)!

According to a survey I read a while ago, 80 percent of businesses fail at their start-up phase (1-5 years), 10 percent could not maintain their growth, 5 percent grow at a very nominal rate, and only 5 percent of businesses actually achieve their objectives. One of the major reasons behind the failure of those businesses is that many of the entrepreneurs/business owners were ill prepared for the challenges faced by a new business.

A new business requires attention, care and responsiveness. It is like a small mustard seed, which you sow in the hope that one day it will grow into a tree. You have to take care of it at every growing stage, like you would a baby.

If neglected or badly cultivated, it invariable yields unfavourable results.

In other words, like the parents of a new baby life changes for ever!

You cannot live the same way you used to live and expect to have a successful business. You cannot go on the same number of holidays, watch the same amount of TV, spend the same hours dog walking or whatever else you enjoyed as an employee and expect to build a successful business!

The initial or start-up phase of any business is the most difficult and attention demanding. If you put in the work now, you can go back and live better than you did before you created your successful business.

Change your lifestyle

Running your own business will require a complete change in lifestyle. You cannot have the same casual attitude for your business as you may have done on your 9-5. I want to reiterate what I said earlier. You have to sacrifice a number of things like holidays, movies, favourite shows, family gatherings, etc. However, it won't be forever; just until the business gets off the ground.

Here are some important tips which you may wish to adopt:

1. Save time and money

It is necessary to reduce your spending activities if you want the best for your business (more on this in a later chapter). Every business requires some level of financial resources, even the ones you start online. The more money you have at your disposal, the better it will be for the business. Save your money and spend less! If you have been spending 6 hours a week watching TV, make do with 2hours. If you spend 6 hours dog walking every week (some people do), go for 2 or get rid of the dog (ouch! Might even save you some money too). If you have been going on two holidays a year, maybe don't go on any for the next 2 years. You need to save your time and money because your business needs attention.

2. Engage in activities that are good for your business

If you are lacking in skills, as mentioned in the previous chapters, get the necessary training before you start your business instead of a holiday expense. Expend more of your spare time on your business. Instead of surfing the internet check for your product suppliers, customers, laws, rules, taxation policies, etc.

3. Be patient

Most people want an overnight success. Viral products/videos/websites rarely happen in practice. Business demands time and patience. Move step by step.

4. Keep Reviewing your daily activities

Maintain an activity log that will help you to fully account for your time. Some time consuming activities may not be non-productive for your business. A daily activity log helps you measure your results against the objectives you set out to achieve. It then gives you the opportunity to change what happens the next day.

Conclusion

Running your own business is not an easy option; it requires a complete change in lifestyle. New businesses in particular require time and patience plus a commitment to the changes. You should stick with your plan and prepare for the long haul. If you get there quicker, then that is all well and good too. Rearrange your daily activities and get the most out of it; then the weeks and months will produce results from those daily actions!

The next chapter throws light on time management as an aid to greater personal and business achievements.

Chapter 5: Time – This is the "Achilles Heel" for most people

After reading the previous chapter, you may be wondering how you could possibly manage your time in relation to your new life of running a business. Usually, most people are concerned about where they are going to get the time to run a business since they feel so flat out with the work. However, every time this question comes up and I start asking how they spend their 'minutes', we soon find 2-5 hours a week they could spend on their businesses. Usually those who are not serious about owning a business give the copout line: "so what time do I have to relax?"

Either you want to start your business or you want to be a complainer and waste your time watching movies and playing cards; time will tell.

In my view, it is not very difficult as long as you are not afraid -

To leave your comfort zone!

If your goal is to run a business with purpose, that generates a constant stream of earning backed with security, then you have to function outside your current area of comfort.

Think about the ability to earn several times more money than your employer pays plus the joy of being able to offer jobs to several others instead of begging for a job for yourself.

However, time becomes a bigger issue, because the way that life is arranged, whenever you plan to do something that takes you out one level to a higher one, there are always many challenges to test your conviction.

If you plan to enjoy, there never seems to be the same amount of obstacles to climb, compared to when you plan to create a long lasting, successful business, with passive income.

Solutions

Given below are solutions to manage your schedule in a more productive way:

1. **Prioritize**

    As mentioned in other parts of the book - Prioritize your tasks which are most urgent. Tasks like reading the newspaper or watching a football game is not so important, whereas tasks such as meeting your official deadlines, attending conferences, etc. are more important. You have to identify the important and unimportant tasks from your daily routine, and then prioritize them accordingly. When you do that you might even find leisure moments more enjoyable because you are not suffering from guilt.

2. Leave current job and take on a less demanding job

If you think that your current job is very hectic and is creating a hurdle towards your goal, then you may consider quitting and finding a job which is less demanding. The purpose is to utilise the time gained on your business, whilst in employment.

3. Work part-time

You can also work part time, if you think that you could no longer manage a full time job. Part time workers usually have more time to spend on their business, as compared to those working full time.

4. **Don't put it off for tomorrow**

   Don't pileup your work, and don't keep pushing your work that you need to do today, into tomorrow. This will help you meet your deadlines, and eliminate stress.

Conclusion

A new business calls for a complete restructuring of the way you spend your time. Valuable time saving lessons can be learnt from what has already been discussed in this chapter.

However action must be taken to ensure you get the results available you.

One more important tip to share - set a definite time to work on your business, and I suggest at least 45 minutes of concentrated, undisturbed time, every single day – this will radically change your achievements!

Chapter 6: Cut Down Your Expenses

As discussed in the preceding chapters, starting your own business is not an easy decision.

There are 3 major areas of restriction when it comes to starting a business while in employment:

- Time
- Information
- Money

We have covered the first two and now I want to deal with the subject of money in a bit more detail.

The reason most people are still in full time employment and not starting a business (assuming that is what they desire to do), is largely due to finance. Either they have huge debts, large mortgages, big loans, credit card issues or are simply living beyond their means. I know of a couple who have been trying to start a business for the past 5 years. They tried saving, but they were always spending all they earned and more. The business needs about $10,000 to start. They would never be able to save when you consider the manner in which they spend. They still buy the same expensive toys for the children; go on the same number of holidays and shop like as and when needed instead of making bulk purchases. The husband is particularly frustrated, but does not know when to put his foot down and let the family know "we are going to have to tighten up for the next 2 years until the business takes off". The spending continues, and so does the frustration.

How to save money for your business?

There is no way out of cutting down your expenses, at least for most people. If you do not cut your expenses, your business will be drained of the life it needs to push forward.

You have to cut your monthly budget in an effort to build your savings. Question is - what can be cut from your monthly household expenses?

Technology and the competitive business environments bring competitive prices for the buyers. You have to review your monthly household expenses periodically to be sure you are getting the best deals.

Here are some of the monthly expenses which you can review, in an effort to save more for your business.

1. Insurance

Compare prices for auto, home, health, business and life insurance. Consolidating at one insurance company could lower your insurance costs. That might mean you'll need to take your business elsewhere and save money. But before you do, be sure you're getting all the discounts you deserve at your current company.

Consider raising your deductible for lower rates. Ask your agent what other discounts you might qualify for. Often, working from home could mean a discount on auto insurance.

2. Financial Fees

Are you still paying a monthly fee even though your bank now offers free checking? Particularly if you have direct deposit, most banks offer some type of free checking. I found I was paying $8 month for only a few services (like free certified checks) that weren't available on the bank's free checking program.

Do you incur ATM fees because your bank's machines are not convenient? It might be as simple as reviewing your current bank's options otherwise consider migrating your account to an Internet bank, especially if earning more interest is important to you.

3. Cable and Satellite Television

Competition in this industry means that new money saving packages are now available. Television and phone service providers are now bundling their services, so consolidating your broadband, phone and TV services at one company may save money.

New customers, whether bundling services or not, usually get the best deals, so it may be necessary to switch providers. Sometimes, threatening to switch will get you a discount. If you're really serious about saving money, consider downgrading your package by cutting out pay cable channels; who on earth can watch 600 channels anyway?

4. Cell Phone

Cell phone companies love to offer free phones to induce sign up additional contractual tenure. But before you renew your contract ask yourself a few questions:

- Do you really need a new phone and what are the hidden costs? (I got my cell phone from E-bay for $30, rather than take the free one and the two-year contract.)
- Are you using all the minutes allotted?
- Are you paying for Internet and texting but not using it enough to justify the cost? Or are you using it so much that another plan might be a better deal?
- Would a cheaper plan or a prepaid cell phone serve you just as well?

5. Telephone

Many people are getting rid of their landlines entirely. However, if you work out of your home, this may not be a feasible option. But, if you have a separate fax line, you might consider discontinuing it. With a scanner/scanner app, you can email documents as PDFs instead of faxing.

Like cable and Internet providers, landline phone service packages keep getting cheaper as the space becomes more competitive. Consider VOIP or cable phone services. If you do stay with your traditional telephone company, be sure you are getting the cheapest long distance service and not paying for services you don't use.

6. Internet Provider

Shopping around for a better package of telephone services might also save you money on your Internet access if you use DSL. But there are many other options for Internet services including cable, satellite and a whole host of wireless Internet options.

The Internet is a telecommuter's lifeline, so do your research first. Be sure if you change service providers the new one will offer the services and reliability your business needs.

7. Refinance Your Home

Refinancing your home can cut your monthly budget expenses significantly, and can sometimes save you hundreds of dollars per month.

Refinancing involves many upfront costs (interest points, taxes, fees, etc.), so it may take several months (or even years) for you to actually realize these savings.

However if you're not planning to stay in the house for long, you could actually lose money on refinancing. Carefully consider the pros and cons of refinancing your home before taking this cost-cutting step.

8. Credit Card Rewards Points

If you have a credit card with rewards points, use them, but use them wisely. Keep in mind that credit card companies offer points to induce you to spend more. So don't pay more (by racking up interest or fees) in order to get rewards points. To accumulate points faster, concentrate spending on the one card that offers the reward you will use (for me that's the one with Home Depot gift cards) rather than spreading your spending among several cards.

Saving rewards points for your dream vacation or another splurge runs the risk of the points expiring or never being used. Using points on a regular basis helps you cut your monthly expenses. Consider using rewards systems that pay cash or offer gift cards that you will actually use.

9. Utility Bills

Like phone and cable industries, your utility company likely has more competition than it once did. Often, you can change gas or electric suppliers for a better price on your energy needs, while still remaining a customer of the same utility company for billing and delivery purposes. However, these other suppliers don't always have a better price so be sure to do some comparison shopping.
Remember, the old-fashioned way to save on utility costs is simply to conserve electricity or waste less water.

10. Credit Card Interest Expense

Monthly interest can be a huge expense for those with a large debt. Making only a minimum payment means the monthly interest eats up most of your payment. Reducing interest can mean more money for paying off debt faster or other expenses.

One way to lower your interest is to simply ask for a lower interest rate. Companies will often oblige to keep your business. If they don't, consider a balance transfer to another card with a better rate. Read the fine print though, as balance transfers sometimes offer rates that go up after a period of time and usually involve fees.

Conclusion

Starting your business requires huge financial input and for a salaried person, it is not easy to save a large pile of money besides meeting daily expenses. In such circumstances, you have to cut down your budget. You don't have to cut your necessities, but you have to find a way to cut down the recurring expenses. The above ten tips will give you an idea that can you save money from your recurring expenses.

Chapter 7: Work Part Time or Start Your Business Part Time

In the preceding chapters, it has been discussed that there are a number of decisions that young entrepreneurs have to make. One of the most important of these is whether you would work part time, or start your business part time.

In this chapter I will be providing you with more information that can help you make an informed choice. You have to be aware that on the job, you are availing certain facilities and have access to certain perks. However, all these benefits may not be available to you while working part time.

Pros and Cons of starting a Part Time Business

In my personal view, you have to start your business part time, even if you are planning to carry on your business full time. Starting on a part-time basis can offer you several advantages like little stress, low financial risks, etc. While working full time, you can rely on the constant income and benefits from your full time job. Furthermore, a constant flow of income helps to grow your business gradually. The stress level is lower when you are doing a full time job rather than doing a full time business.

In spite of certain advantages, the part time path of doing business also brings certain pitfalls. It can leave you with less time to market, strategize and build a clientele. Clients may feel you're not offering adequate customer service. You also run the risk of burning out. Holding down a full-time job while running a part-time business can leave you with little, if any, leisure time, and your personal life may suffer as a result.

I am of the view that part time business while doing full time job is good, but I never said that it is an easy task. You have to manage a number of things all alone. You'll need to have excellent time-management skills, strong self-discipline, and support from family and friends.

While doing a part time business, don't think that you are doing a full time job, therefore you don't have to put in effort on your part time business. You have to work hard in your part time business, so that you can make it a full time career for yourself.

Tips for Making your Decision

I know it is not easy for you to decide which path to go. Whether to start part-time or full-time is a decision only you can make. Whichever route you take, the secret to success is an honest assessment of your resources, your commitment level and the support systems you have in place. With those factors firmly in mind, you will be able to make the right choice. There are a few tips which will help you to decide:

1. Analyse the Market

If you find there is an unmet need for your product or service, no major competition and a ready supply of eager customers, then starting full-time might be the best plan. On the other hand, if you find the market won't support a full-time business, but might someday with proper marketing and development, then it is probably best to start part-time. Investigate the competition in your industry, the economy in your area, the demographic breakdown of your client base and the availability of potential customers.

For example, if you are planning to start a management training firm, then you have to check how many are already working in the locality, their clientele numbers, revenues and expenses. You have to do pertinent homework before going for it.

2. Write a Business Plan

You have to write a comprehensive business plan. Make market projections and set goals for yourself based on these findings. It gives you a view of the long-range possibilities and keeps the business on track. Part-timers should write a business plan too, as it will help your transition to full-time later on.

3. Evaluate Your Finances

Whether, you are starting a full time or part time business, you have to evaluate your finances. If you have decided to start as full time, then according to experts, you have to put aside enough money to live on for at least six months. You also have to decide how much you want to pour in your business and from where you will get your finances. Either it is your family, friends or some bank, financial institutes, etc. Your business may have an impact on your family, so you have to check whether the family members' salaries are enough to support your family while you launch a business full-time.

If you're leaning toward starting part-time, then you have more leverage. You have to do a complete financial analysis in order to know when your business is making enough money that you can quit your day job. A good rule of thumb is to wait until your part-time business is generating income equivalent to at least 30 percent of your current salary from your full-time job.

4. Bring Your Family into the Process
(More on this subject in the next chapter)
You should not forget that your family is also a stake holder, so don't ignore them when making your decision to start your business.

You have to know that in both cases, whether you start part time or full time, at the initial level it requires sacrifices. You have to check under which circumstances your family members support you. Do they understand the sacrifices that full-time and part-time businesses will require? Make sure they know that they can discuss any objections or worries they have with you. Then work together to develop practical solutions to the problems you foresee. Also, lay ground rules for the part-time business. For instance, agree not to work on Sunday afternoons, or not to discuss business at the dinner table.

5. Decide it sensibly
You have to reassess your skills and abilities then you have to decide it on your own. If the idea of taking the full-time business plunge keeps you awake at night, then perhaps a part-time business is best. On the other hand, if you think that you could not carry on a full

time job and you want to do your business without taking care of circumstances, then you are good to do your full time business.

Conclusion

Whether to start part-time or full-time is a decision only you can make. You have to check all the pros and cons of both routes and you should take the route which is most suitable for you. Assess the effects of both a part-time and a full-time business on your life. You'll most likely be working evenings, weekends and lunch hours, if not your holidays, sick days and vacation time, too. This is the kind of commitment you will need to make if you expect your business to succeed.

Chapter 8: Role of the Family in Your Business Start-up

One of the most unfortunate and common situations that young entrepreneurs face is unsupportive family. While your friendships can be replaced, family are here to stay. Living with (literally or not) parents or siblings who do not understand, or simply refuse to support your entrepreneurial aspirations, can often be the breaking point for many early-stage entrepreneurs.

Your family (spouse, children, parents, etc.) can help and support you in starting your business, or they can sabotage your business dreams. Starting a business can drain the family's bank account, require working long hours away from home, and change your lifestyle to the extent to which your vacations and health insurance are temporarily lost on account of the Start-Up. Stress can lead to disagreements that can cause separation and divorce - if not managed well. Whilst I did not find statistical data tracking business start-ups as a direct cause of divorce, we all know that it can and does happen.

According to a recent survey, lack of health insurance, time management and the great amount of energy required to run a business emanate problems to budding entrepreneurs. Some business owners mentioned that at business start-up, the long hours involved and "sometimes not even taking time to sleep!" caused major distress which disturbed their work life balance.

Incidentally families find themselves making unpalatable sacrifices especially at the Start up - Growth stages of the business. These sacrifices can create animosity with an unsympathetic spouse, and "the stress definitely trickles down to everyone".

How to move your family along a paradigm shift

If you are experiencing resentment or lack of support from your family; ask the following questions:

- What is their real reason for the lack of support?
- Are they unclear about what I am doing?
- Are they thinking about my past business failures?
- Do they know of others who have failed in business?
- Do they doubt my ability, due to age, lack of experience, or preconceived notions about what they think I can or can't do?

It's very important to put your own feelings aside for a moment and look at your situation objectively. Once you understand the underlying reasons, face the pessimists directly with a loving confrontation or a plea for understanding.

Once you understand your family's motivations, the next step is to launch your own family PR campaign. No, this is not a joke.

Anyone who has ever been in this horrible situation knows how difficult these circumstances can be. Hopefully, the following suggestions will help you overcome any bad family vibes you may be receiving.

1. Communication
Bring your success stories home. Send your family copies of client letters or emails that praise your work. Show them a customer's check for payment. Share any media articles about your company with them. Tack them up on the refrigerator or bulletin board – somewhere visible to everyone in the house. Let them know how happy you are about the business. Seeing you happy is a testimony they could one day enjoy!

2. Convince your Friends & Relatives

Discuss your endeavour with their friends who understand the entrepreneur's journey. Let other people put a little pressure on your family to cut you some slack and show you the respect you deserve for what you are doing. Unfortunately, friends or respected peers are often more likely to recognize your achievements publicly than your family is. Despite how close you might be, it's not uncommon for people to need outside opinions to really open up their perspective – particularly about their own spouse or children.

3. Maintain a healthy Work-life balance

Be sure to avoid neglecting family responsibilities because of your business, whether that includes family gatherings or doing the dishes. Be your own person, your own boss, but do your best to show your family that they still hold an important place in your life.

Find the most nurturing and supportive person in your family – your mother, father, uncle, grandmother – whoever is most sympathetic to your overall happiness. Let this person be your campaigner. Run your ideas by them and take on their suggestions!

4. Sell them the dreams
Collect a few stories about people like you who created successful companies. Whether it is the corner grocer or one of the entrepreneurial giants, know their stories well, particularly the vital facts: How old they were when they started, their experience, their family's support (or lack of), their resources, and their current success.

5. Don't share business problems at the dinner table unless your family probe for it!
Avoid sharing business problems or frustrations with them. If they really aren't

supportive of your venture, your mishaps will only fuel their desire to intervene further, or proclaim that they "told you so."

6. Get them involved in doing some of the research

Show them that you have researched your business and have a clear understanding of your options, environment, and chances of success. If you are uncertain about your chances, be honest with them and tell them that despite your own doubts you feel that the experience will be well worth any potential failure. After all, the best way entrepreneurs learn about business is by being in business. You can also get them involved in doing some of the research for your business. People can be less critical when involved in the decision making process.

7. Celebrate the milestones

Celebrate the milestones with your family like registration of your business, sale of products, etc. Involve your family in each and every celebratory moment.

Conclusion

You can choose your friends but you cannot choose your family. Realise that some business ventures fail at the very early stages because of lack of family support. Therefore, you have to involve your family if they are integral to your existence.

Communication is the most powerful tool. Tell them what you want to achieve and how. Never forget to reaffirm your desire for their support!

Chapter 9: The Business Plan

The business plan is a road map for your business, in writing. You sometimes need to write the business plan to obtain finance from banks or any other financial institute, and it may also be an investment condition. Whatever the reason I encourage you to write a business plan before you start running your business.

Writing a business plan will broaden your vision and enable you to think through common business blind spots!

In the light of preceding chapters, I assumed you have done your homework and have generated some content toward your business plan.
Now it is time for you to put pen to paper so to speak.

The Business Plan

Generally speaking, most comprehensive business plans have the same information in them. They may have been given other titles but the basic format and requirements are similar. Hence the template I am giving you may not be the exact format you may have received from your local business adviser or accountant but the information within it will be the same. Also the format I am giving you has been tried and tested and I have personally used it to raise thousands for many of my clients.

The Five Parts of a Business Plan

Think about your hand. It has five fingers, right (hopefully)? Or just imagine you have five fingers. In the same way I want you to know that there are five parts to a business plan:

1. The Summary; also called "Executive

Summary" or "Introduction"

2. The Marketing Plan

3. Operations Plan

4. Financial Plan

5. Appendices

These are the names I have used and it is easy for me to remember them. If at the end of the book you feel you want to call them something else then feel free to do so. The only proviso is that if you are trying to reach other people with the plan, they need to be familiar with or understand the terms you give the plan.

What Each Title Stands for:

1. **The Marketing Plan** – "What I Want to Do" - What type of business are you wanting to start?
What market do you want to start your business in? Who do you want to cater to? Etc.

2. **The Operation Plan** – "How I Am Going to Do It" – What kind of business structure do I need for this enterprise? Who do I need to network with? Do I need a mentor? Etc.

3. **The Financial Plan** – "What It Will Cost to Do It" - What are the costs of production, cost of sales or monthly expenses? How much profit will the business make in 12 months? Etc.

4. **Appendices** – "Additional Supportive Information" - like letters of intent, letters of recommendation, CV etc.

5. **The final part which is the first one or two pages of your plan is the "Summary" or "Executive Summary".** Which is the summary of all the above 4 (Marketing Plan, Operations Plan, Financial Plan and Appendices). The general advice given is that this section must be written last and I agree to that. You will understand more as we build up the business plan.

Other components to consider:
Define Your Target Market

Market analysis provides you an indication of the growth potential within the industry, which allows you to develop your own estimates for the future of your business. Begin your analysis by defining the market in terms of

88

size, structure, growth prospects, trends and sales potential.

The total aggregate sales of your competitors will provide you with a fairly accurate estimate of the total potential market.

Once the size of the market has been determined, the next step is to define your own target market **(Niche)**. The target market narrows down the total market by concentrating on segmentation factors that determine the total addressable market, or the total number of users within the sphere of the business's influence. The segmentation factors can be geographic, customer attributes or product-oriented.

Position Your Business

A company's strategic position is affected by a number of variables that are closely tied to the motivations and requirements of target customers, as well as the actions of primary competitors. Before a product can be positioned, you need to answer several strategic questions such as:

1. How are your competitors positioning themselves?
2. What specific attributes does your product have that your competitors' don't?
3. What customer needs does your product fulfil?

Once you've answered your strategic questions based on research of the market, you can then begin to develop your positioning strategy and illustrate that in your business plan.

A positioning statement for a business plan doesn't have to be long or elaborate. It should merely point out exactly how you want your product perceived by both customers and the competition.

Pricing

How you price your product is important because it will have a direct effect on the success of your business. You have to be clear about your pricing strategy, and you must write it in your business plan. You must be aware of the basic principles of pricing which should never be overlooked:
1. Price of the product/service must cover all costs.
2. The only way to (profitably) lower the price is to lower the cost of production.

Identify and Analyse Your Competition

The competitive analysis is a statement of the business strategy and how it relates to the competition. The purpose of the competitive analysis is to determine the strengths and weaknesses of the competitors within your market, strategies that will provide you with a distinct advantage, the barriers that can be developed in order to prevent competition from entering your market, and any weaknesses that can be exploited within the product development cycle.

Conclusion.

Your business plan must be flexible to enough to accommodate new finding and changes in the market place.
It must be more of a workable plan than a string of information. The usability of your plan will be of an immense value to your future success!
Please Click Here to my complete book on Business Planning!

Chapter 10: Go Cold Turkey

I have come to the conclusion that many people will never start their own business unless the following happens:
Get fired
Laid off
Reach retirement age
Go Cold Turkey

The most difficult of all four is to go cold turkey. Meaning; just quit your job as though you have been fired. Whether you have enough money or not just quit, whether you feel ready or not just quit, whether everyone agrees with you or not just quit.

In reality that is the only time some people will actually start otherwise what will happen is people staying within their comfort zone or going from one job to another!

Transitioning from a traditional job to working from home or starting your own business can be scary enough and you need all the push you can get.

Going cold turkey is you pushing yourself over into what you really believe you ought to be doing!

There are 10 very useful tips which you could adopt before quitting your job and starting your own business.

1. Make up your mind

Be persuaded that whatever happens, you will not retreat. Prepare a schedule that states when you will quit your job and when you will start your own business.

2. Check your Homework

You don't have to be hasty in your decisions.

You should cross check that you have completed your homework and have developed a roadmap for the future business that includes market niche, product ideas, suppliers, potential customers, products/services, rules, policies and procedures. Don't make the decisions based on vague data, instead be precise and specific.

3. Clarify your Ambiguities

Be clear minded and focused. Don't indulge yourself in the thoughts which distract your attention. Get yourself cleared from all the ambiguities and continually consider the success of the business you are about to start.

4. Don't be oversensitive

You have to look toward your goal and what you are going to achieve, rather than what you are going to miss.

If you think too much about your jobs and the benefits you are getting from your job, you may not able to quit. You have to understand that there is always an opportunity cost attach to every decision.

5. **Involve your family and friends**

   Don't take your decisions in isolation. Consult your family and friends, and check what they have to say about your decision. Communicate with your family, and consider their views and opinions as well while making a decision. You may also take advice from a consultant or a friend who is already doing his/her own business.

6. **Leave with Dignity**

   When you quit your job for your own business, leave with dignity. Leaving with dignity and honour is not only an ethical and moral responsibility every employee has, but you have to keep it in mind that you are going to be an entrepreneur and your current employer may be your future client. Therefore, you have to keep all aspects in mind and quit your job within ethical and moral and contractual limits.

7. Save your Finances

You have to evaluate your finances in order to know if you have ample resources for next 5-6 months, without getting any earnings from your business. You have to put aside enough money to live on for at least six months. You also have to keep in mind that you should not pour all your savings into your business, but instead consider financing from alternative sources like family and friends rather than going to financial institutions for loans.

8. **It's not a Bed of Roses**

   Whatever you have decided, you shall know that it is not an easy task you are going to do. You have to prepare yourself that you may not get an early success, but you have to make a commitment to yourself that you will not retreat. You have to teach yourself by learning from the failure.

9. **Equip yourself well**

   You must know that you are going to war and you have to prepare yourself accordingly. You have to sharpen your skills, knowledge and abilities. Equip yourself with the modern trends of management and the skills required to be an entrepreneur and to win the war.

10. **Think about the Success**

Don't get disappointed with the small failures; think about the successes that are yet to come. Don't repent over losing your job, but think that in future, with the growth of your business, you will be able to hire a number of employees. Don't take the temporary financial problems to heart; think about the living style that is yet to come.

Conclusion

Most people think about doing their own business, but few of them get success and start their own business. Research shows that such employees, who reached the mid-career level could not start their own business. The major reason behind this phenomenon is that the employees at the mid-career level think that they could not quit their job, as they have to look after their family, loans, bills, household expenses, etc. In fact, it is not so.

Whenever you decide to start your business, you have to do it with strong footings. You have to write a road map and act according to that. You should be realistic and well aware of the problems that you may have to face in the future. In such situations, you should not be disappointed. You should be aware that every dark cloud has a silver lining. You should think about your success, business growth and luxurious life style that is just one step ahead from you.

Final Chapter

It has been noted that 80% of people who read a book or attend a training program fail to experience any change because they simply will not put what they have learned into practice.

Of the remaining 20%, 80% of them will try it for a while and if they face any difficulty they give up. The final 20% of the remaining 20% will actually practice and persevere with what they have learned and many will succeed to millionaire status.

The question is not whether you agree with everything written in this book, but whether you will put into practice the things you read in this book that you agreed with!

Someone said that if you are not planning then you are planning to fail. I want to encourage you to put into practice all the aspects of the book you found interesting and know that as you actualise a plan, you will have great results.

I sincerely hope that you will contact me with good news of your business success so that we can celebrate "You" together.

I wish you all the best!

Boomy Tokan

T: +44 7932 394620
E: boomy@startyourownbusinessacademy.com
W: startyourownbusinessacademy.com
#: @boomybizbooks

Thank you so much for reading my book. I hope you really liked it. As you probably know, many people look at the reviews on Amazon before they decide to purchase a book. If you liked the book, **could you please take a minute** *to leave a review with your feedback? 60 seconds is all I'm asking for, and it would mean the world to me.*
Thank you so much,
Boomy Tokan,
T: +44 7932 394620
E: boomy@startyourownbusinessacademy.com
W: startyourownbusinessacademy.com
#: @boomybizbooks

FREE Bonus

How To Start Your Own Business In 30 Days"

Hey ... If you would like to learn how to start and run a "High Performance" business;

then download this FREE guide. It will also show you how to start making money from your business within 30 Days!

"How To Start Your Own Business In 30 Days"

Copy and paste in your browser:
www.startyourownbusinessacademy.com/freedownload1

Enjoy

Other Books by Boomy Tokan

"How To Write Your First Business Plan": With Outline and Templates Book (First Timer's Guide:)

Introduction & Chapter 1
In this book, I am going to teach you how to write two (2) types of business plans. The first one is a Comprehensive Business Plan Template and the second, a Power Point Business Plan. (I'll explain more in a moment)

Let me start by making two statements:

If you are just starting out in business, you need a business plan because of all the instructions and knowledge you will gain from going through education.

Writing a business plan is easy; at least it is easier than most people think. The problem lie in the manner business plans are perceived and portrayed by many institutions. Most have made the process intimidating for those who want to have a plan but do not want to be bothered with the plethora of business jargons that have been overemphasized in the business plan writing process.

My advice is - dispense with frivolities and write a well researched plan, the rest are details! The most important element of a business plan is the content not the jargon!

Ok let's get started!

The Comprehensive Business Plan Template

Generally speaking, most comprehensive business plans have the same information in them. They may have been given other titles but the basic format and requirements are similar. Hence the template I am giving you may not be the exact format you may have received from your local business adviser or accountant but the information within it will be the same. Also the format I am giving you has been tried and tested and I have personally used it to raise thousands for many of my clients.

The Five Parts of a Business Plan

Think about your hand. It has five fingers, right (hopefully)? Or just imagine you have five fingers. In the same way I want you to know that there are five parts to a business plan:

1. The Summary; also called "Executive Summary" or "Introduction"

2. The Marketing Plan

3. Operations Plan

4. Financial Plan

5. Appendices

These are the names I have used and it is easy for me to remember them. If at the end of the book you feel you want to call them something else then feel free to do so. The only proviso is that if you are trying to reach other people with the plan, they need to be familiar with or understand the terms you give the plan.

What Does Each Name Stand For:

1. **The Marketing Plan** – "What I Want To Do" - What type of business are you wanting to start?

What market do you want to start your business in? Who do you want to cater to?

2. **The Operation Plan** – "How I Am Going To Do It" – What kind of business structure do I need for this enterprise? Who do I need to network with? Do I need a mentor?

3. **The Financial Plan** – "What It Will Cost To Do It" - What are the costs of production, cost of sales or monthly expenses? How much profit will the business make in 12 months?

4. **Appendices** – "Additional Supportive Information" - like letters of intent, letters of recommendations, CV etc

5. **The final part which is the first one or two pages of your plan is the "Summary" or "Executive Summary".** Which is the summary of all the above 4 (Marketing Plan, Operations Plan, Financial Plan and Appendices). The general advice given is that this section must be written last and I agree to that. You will understand more as we build up the business plan.

Once you understand this then you are ready to progress to the next stage. ....

Book Title: Business Funding Secrets: *How To Get Small Business Loans, Crowd Funding, Loans From Peer To Peer Lending, Government Grants and Personal Funding Ideas; Book*

If you want to know the truth about raising money for your business this book is for you.

If you are having a tough time raising the money you want for your business this book is for you too.

If you are not sure where to go to get the kind of funding you need for your business this book is just what you need.

After many years of helping businesses of various kinds raise the money they want, I have laid out in print all that you need to know about raising money for your start-up business! .

Read Introduction & Chapter 1
Introduction

I want to start by making a bold statement "There is more funding available than needed by Start-up Businesses"

Many start-up businesses convince themselves that the reason why it is difficult to get the money they need is because of scarcity. Nothing could be so far from the truth. Let me give you an example. When I worked for an organisation that gave loans to start-up businesses, they always had money for the businesses they believed would succeed and they usually rejected and gave a hard time to those businesses they felt would under-perform.

The problem is not scarcity but the lack of understanding the psychology for raising business finances.

Facts

"Business money is out there to be claimed, yet every year we receive stories of piles of cash sitting in accounts and not being invested. It's not because you don't need the cash, but it's because navigating through the grants jungle can have you wishing you still

had your good job back".
http://www.startups.co.uk/grants-for-starting-a-business.html

Many people come to a raising finances seminar and at the back of their minds is this statement, "Give me the list of funders and I'll be on my way." The truth is that if you had a list of funders without understanding, it will be like giving a learner driver a Ferrari sports car. Occasionally they will drive the car on the road but they are more likely to crash than to survive the next 10 miles.

Understanding how to approach funders, knowing how to turbo-charge your business idea, presenting yourself well and finding solutions to all the hindrances on the way are much more important than having a long list of funding sources alone. So I have left that to the final part of the chapter. That is where I will tell you the various sources of funding and their requirements.

What the major players say:

Huw Morgan, Head of Business Banking for SMEs at HSBC Commercial Banking UK, agrees. He says HSBC looks at each business on a case-by-case basis when deciding whether to lend. "When making lending decisions we are looking to support firms with good cash flow management, a strong balance sheet, a sound business plan, a well-balanced management team, a good business record, and who are looking to develop and grow."

Neil Mackay of Advantage Business Angels suggests "you need to put some real effort into preparing a business plan: not a consultant template driven one but a well thought out document. Particular emphasis should be placed on sales and the plan should be less than 10 pages of A4".
http://www.sage.co.uk/business-potential/start-your-business/how-to-raise-finance-for-your-business.html

This book is written to help start-up and other newly established businesses understand the intricacies of raising money and position them to be able to leverage their ideas better and attract the required funding.

For easy reference I have split the book into 5 key sections:

1.   Answers to common, sensible questions about raising money for their business

2.   Why start-up fails to get the funding they require and the necessary solutions

3.   How to make your business fundable

4.   Understanding the psychology of investors

5.   Where is the money?

I have endeavoured to make this book as practical as possible, not leaving out any information that can be of help. Over the years I have helped many businesses raise finances from hundreds to thousands of dollars. Therefore my desire is that this book will help you along your journey to raising finances. The most important message I want to pass on to you as you begin reading the book is – Take Action Today!

Chapter 1: Answers to Common, Sensible Questions about Raising Money for Your Business

Anyone who has raised any amount of money for a business understands the pressure and the amount of time it can take to actually get the money in the bank. What I want to do first is to answer some of the common questions about raising money for your business:

1. How long does it take to get the money?: In every group I have delivered a lecture on raising money someone always asks me how long it takes from application process to receiving money from the bank. Unless you already have a great credit score and you are going to a bank that likes your account, then the average wait time is anywhere between 3-18 months. Somebody says, "What?" Yes 3-18 months! In some cases, it can even take over two years.

Knowing this information is really important because it means you need to plan in advance for your funding drive. Many people put themselves under pressure by applying for money exactly when they need it. Funders are very wary of people under such pressures because they appear to lack the ability to plan ahead and if that is the case how could they possibly plan for a business!

2. Does a good idea guarantee or equate to getting funding? No. What guarantees getting the funds you need is a good idea that is presented well. A good idea alone may get you nothing. What many new businesses may not know is that there are always many good ideas at the same time! I know by experience that everyone thinks they have the best idea and rightly so, otherwise you will have no imputes to go out and get the funding you need. But the reality is that some funders can have in excess of 1000 applications every month!

3. Do I need to get funders to sign a confidentiality agreement? A few years ago I met with a man called John Oram who produces valve music amplifiers; expensive stuff!. In a life changing conversation, he told me that when he gets an idea it seems to come in a complete package. He also told me that he believes he is not the only one that gets the same idea at the same time. I asked him how he knew he was not the only one that had the same idea. His answer was shocking. He said that on many occasions he worked with people from different countries and they seemed to know intricate details of equipment that had never been manufactured. When he asked them how they got the idea the time and date mentions was the exact time and date he also received the idea! Amazing I told him that divine download was from GOD. If people separated by 100's miles can have the same ideas, you can begin to understand the problem with confidentiality agreements. Some else can walk into the same funder with an idea similar to yours. Any way; funders hate to sign such documents. It puts them in a difficult position. To be frank with you, I will never sign such an agreement and when I was working for an advisory agency, we were told never to sign them because it could result in lawsuits.

Don't worry about the bad stories you hear of someone infringing another person's copyright; it only happens on rare occasions. If you think someone is likely to steal your idea do not even approach the person for funding!

4. How many meetings would I have to go to before I get the money? You will have has many that are necessary. But if you follow the ideas in this book you should reduce the number of meeting to the minimum. Honestly the number of meetings has to be judged on a case by case basis.

Initially there will be a flurry of going back and forth because there is likely to be issues the funders are not pleased with.

I must tell you this in my experience of placing business plans to funders I have never come across a complete business plan. I have come across very good business plans but never satisfied with every single detail of the plan. Besides you need to get used to the fact that all funders have different requirements and you will need to tailor your plan to their rules.

5. How many funders would I need to approach? One answer is as many as possible. The other is if you do your research properly an average of 5-10 funders should do it. Do your research and then choose a few that are likely to fund your idea. If I go to a funder that is likely to fund my type of business and they reject my application, they would likely give reasons for doing so and if I take onboard their suggestions – I increase my chances all the way! Raising money is not pop lunch but a strategic approach is essential!

6. How long should my business plan be? There is no hard and fast rule as to the length of a business plan. However the Business Plan must look the part! Meaning if you are looking for $30,000 it must be obvious to the funders simply by the physical appearance or electronic copy of the plan that it is worth what is being sort! So here are some guiding principles in my opinion: if you want to raise $5000 I suggest at least a 12 page plan; raising $10,000, I suggest at least 15-

20pages; raising $20,000 – $50,000 I suggest at least 25-50pages; raising $100,000, I suggest at least 100pages. I hope you get the picture. No one in their right mind will give $100,000 from a one or two page business plan unless you are Alan Sugar or Richard Branson!

"70 Public Speaking Tips"

Has been written to give individuals the tools and techniques to overcome the fear that limits them from delivering great speeches. **Boomy Tokan** reveals the how-to's of effective Public Speaking, and reveals how anyone can learn and implement them.
For all who need to make presentations in the workplace, at school or an event and expects someone to listen, ***70 Public Speaking Tips provides an insider's guide on how to***

present effectively
You will receive the exact steps needed to create a speech that will keep your audience engaged. The book is easy to follow, inspiring to read and designed to motivate you to become the best speaker you never thought you could be!

Topics covered include:
- Why You Need This Skill
- **Why some people have the fear of speaking in public. – It's origin and development**
- Psychology of public speaking (Part 1) - The internal dialogue of the person that hates public speaking.
- **Psychology of public speaking (Part 2) - The internal dialogue of the 'Successful' public speaker**
- How to overcome fear, stage fright and shyness of Public Speaking
- **Public Speaking exercises that will change you into a great speaker forever**
- 10 Tips that will help you captivate an audience
- **The Ultimate Public Speaking Preparation 'The 7 Most Do's' – How to prepare**
- How to choose an engaging topic and incorporate relevant stories
- Foods **which aid better Public Speaking**
- The Biggest Secret is the 'Secret of Practicing'

Read Introduction & Chapter 1
Introduction

The ability to speak in public confidently, articulately, and in a manner that enables others to completely comprehend what has been said, is of immense value to everyone who possesses it!

It was not until I was in college that it dawned on me that I had mastered public speaking to a proficient level.

I noticed that every time the tutor told us we had an assignment that would require a presentation, 99% of the class would complain and lobby the tutor to scrap the presentation aspect of the course work. I often sat there wondering why this took place all the time. It dawned on me that most of the students hated public speaking and, as the famous line goes, most people fear public speaking more than they fear death!

If this is your sentiment, I am about to change your fear into confidence for good.

Read on!

Once I realized my perception about the students was correct, I went about making my life easier! From that day, whenever we had course work that required a presentation, I would tell my group: "You guys do all the work. When it is ready, give it to me and I'll make the presentation." They would look so relieved! And so they would do all the work and I would read the report and present it. I thought this was a win-win deal; I got out of doing all the research and they got off doing the presenting!

It was only as I grew older that I realized we both lost. I did not learn administration and research in my earlier academic career (something I had to re-learn later in life), and they failed to master their fear of public speaking!

The other thing I began to grasp was that, contrary to what many people believe, public speaking can be learnt by EVERYONE! Rather than master the art of public speaking, many have mastered the art of public speaking "avoidance."

One of the fundamentals of this book is to let you know that if you want the fear and anxiety of public speaking to be completely eliminated, eradicated and extinguished from your life; the only way is to PRACTICE, PRACTICE, PRACTICE.

No amount of books you read (including mine) can replace practice. Books teach you methods and techniques. A book can work on changing your mind-set towards a given subject and can guide you into a reality that can motivate you to start practicing. However, if you do not practice, it is highly unlikely that you will ever conquer the fear and become a master of this skill.

Many people think the ability to speak publically will just fall on them like rain! For an exceptional few, yes, maybe, but for the majority of us, you need to learn it.

Public speaking is a skill, like driving. It can be learnt!

So, welcome to "70 Public Speaking Tips", where you will discover numerous methods, teachings, techniques and opportunities to practice the art of Public Speaking, and thereby reap all the benefits and advantages it can bring you!

Your public awaits...!

Enjoy

"I will pay more for a person who has good public speaking abilities" - Warren Buffet

Chapter One: Why You Need This Skill

As I alluded to in the introduction, public speaking is a skill, and because of that, anyone who is determined and willing can acquire it. Just as driving is a skill that anyone can get, so is public speaking. To consider that not anyone can speak publically is to say not everyone can drive. In reality, we know that anyone can drive, even if they have to take their tests 7, 10 or even 20 times and never give up. The reason you don't see many people driving is that if they fail to pass the test once or twice, most people give up.

My wife saw no reason to go on for yet another test after failing twice. But when we moved to an area where everyone needed to be mobile; she was so determined that she passed on the fifth attempt.

What most people do is that if they have a bad experience in public speaking, they stop doing it. The longer they leave it, the more they are reluctant to attempt it further, and it goes on like that until many live in constant fear. I have seen even people of colour go red when they are called to speak publically. Many would plead and beg not to be called to speak, even to a small audience.

But according to Warren Buffet, he will pay more to people who have good public speaking skills!

I want to give 3 reasons why you must be determined to acquire this skill.

#Tip 1
It creates the opportunity to impart others. Most people I have met have one heart cry, and that is the desire to impart others with what they know. While you are able to do this one-to-one, you can also do this one-to-many. If you are a great public speaker, you can impart many people at the same time. Either through a workshop, or seminar, or an event.

If you are not willing to learn this skill, your reach in life will be limited. Who wants to die with any regrets? Think about this—no matter how old you are now, project to the time you will be going to meet your Maker; who wants to know they could have impacted 1000 people, yet they only impacted 10 people because they did not learn a skill?

You are too important, plus, you know too much, and people need to hear from you. The sad truth is that people who are not as knowledgeable as you are, or possess less intellectual capabilities, are reaching people with their mediocre message, but you are still hugging your seat.

It is time for you to let your light shine and start delivering what you know to people who need to hear from you one-to-one, or in small or large groups!

#Tip 2

It creates more job and business opportunities. It will amaze you how many people have passed on great opportunities just because they knew it would involve some kind of public speaking. Sadly, what those people do not realise is that public speaking is one of the most fun, most rewarding, most personally satisfying activities you can ever be engaged in.

Did you know that the higher up the echelon of success you are, the more likely you will give presentations. This may be in the boardroom or large events.

If you avoid public speaking, you are basically single-headedly sabotaging your own career!

I even read at some point that people did not attend job interviews, even though they needed a job; just because they hated public speaking!

When it comes to public speaking, many lose sleep over their natural voice or accent. You will be understood if you deliver content that is relevant, from your heart, and meet the needs of people confidently and at a good pace.

Those who can communicate publically have a better selection of choices when it comes to careers and other opportunities. You can do it, too. You can learn and be better at public speaking.

#Tip 3
It creates the opportunity for increased revenue. Apart from the job prospects we discussed above, and their related salaries and responsibilities, there are other opportunities open to someone who can speak on any subject confidently.

It is not uncommon for well-known speakers to earn in excess of $50,000 a day to speak publically. According to Les Brown, he earned nearly $500,000 for a one day speaking engagement!

Some of these opportunities are:

- Running your own seminars
- Speaking as a guest at someone's seminar
- Guest speaking at an event
- Being on a panel with other speakers
- Video interviews

I hope I have managed to persuade you of the need to learn this vital skill. As we proceed further into the book, I want you to be determined that you will put into practice what you learn!

Action Point.
Be determined to practice what you learn from this book!

[Buy This Book On Amazon](#)

The Bad Girls Of The Bible *- 7 Most Infamous*

Ever wondered why some people are just – bad? In this book you will discover some well-known characters and other obscure ones that can teach you life lessons for the 21st Century. This book will educate and inspire you!

Read Introduction & Chapter 1
Bad Girls - Introduction

As I was driving to church one Sunday morning with the family, trying to arrive as early as we could, we were caught behind yet another set of traffic lights. I decided to take my mind off the hassle of traffic and focus on other things.

Suddenly, I started wondering about some of the most brutal women in the Bible. Since I love Bible quizzes I asked my wife to name some. There were the obvious ones of course, like Jezebel, but then the not so obvious characters like Athaliah, Micah's mother, who did more evil than even some of the most infamous biblical characters.

I began to think of penning this information into a book. This has taken a while, but here is the result. My aim is that you learn the lessons taught by the HOLY SPIRIT as you read through this book.

I also want you to remember two passages of the Bible.

We are told in 1 Corinthians 10:11,"**These things happened to them as examples and were written down as warnings for us, on whom the fulfilment of the ages has come.**"

And in **2 Timothy 2:15** the Bible says," **Do your best to present yourself to God as**

one approved, a workman who does not need to be ashamed and who correctly handles the word of truth."

I pray that this book will prepare you for a glorious future in CHRIST JESUS.

Remain blessed!

Enjoy!

Chapter One: Athaliah

Who is Athaliah?

Athaliah stood in a class all alone as one of the most vicious, cold-hearted killers in the Bible. Her actions had no bounds regarding age as she ravaged the kingdom in her effort to obliterate GOD'S will and establish her own!

Let's pick up the story about her in 2 Kings 8:26 which says:

Ahaziah was twenty-two years old when he became king, and he reigned in Jerusalem one year. His mother's name was Athaliah, a granddaughter of Omri king of Israel, So Jehoram marries Athaliah (house of Omri who was Ahab's father).They conceive a son called

Ahaziah, so Athaliah automatically becomes the Queen.

Let us look further at the origin of the whole family and the wickedness of Omri and Ahab.Omri came to power by assassinating the ruling king and in an effort to consolidate the strength of the nation; Ahab married Jezebel, the daughter of Ethbaal, who was King of the Sidonians. This relationship between Ahab and Jezebel produced Athaliah.

This is how the Bible describes Omri in 1 Kings 16:25-26:

^{25} But Omri did evil in the eyes of the Lord and sinned more than all those before him.^{26} He walked in all the ways of Jeroboam son of Nebat and in his sin, which he had caused Israel to commit, so that they provoked the Lord, the God of Israel, to anger by their worthless idols.

This is how the Bible describes Ahab in 1 Kings 16:30-33:

^{30} Ahab son of Omri did more evil in the eyes of the Lord than any of those before him.^{31} He not only considered it trivial to commit the sins of Jeroboam son of Nebat, but he also married Jezebel daughter of Ethbaal king of the

*Sidonians, and began to serve Baal and worship him.*³² *He set up an altar for Baal in the temple of Baal that he built in Samaria.*³³ *Ahab also made an Asherah pole and did more to provoke the Lord, the God of Israel, to anger than all the kings of Israel before him.*

This is how the Bible describes her own husband Jehoram in 2 Chronicles 22:13:

¹³ *But you have walked in the ways of the kings of Israel, and you have led Judah and the people of Jerusalem to prostitute themselves, just as the house of Ahab did. You have also murdered your own brothers, members of your father's house, men who were better than you.*

As we read about the household in which Athaliah was born, along with the marriage she had with Jehoram, it was almost expected that she would become evil; the only surprise was why she waited so long to show who she really was!

What did Athaliah do to make her one of the most infamous?

1. **She planned the destruction of GOD's ruling family.** *When Athaliah the mother of*

Ahaziah saw that her son was dead, she proceeded to destroy the whole royal family of the house of Judah. **2 Chronicles 22:10**

This action ranks as one of the most offensive and audacious. The Bible does not tell us the number of people she actually murdered, but it could have been as many as 300 people who could qualify for kingship when we reference back to the lineage of the male relatives of David.

The consequences of her actions could have impacted the coming of the Messiah. How? JESUS had to come from the family line of David, and if Athaliah had succeeded, there would have been no Jesus! In effect, her actions were perceivable just as evil as Herod's who orchestrated the killing of many children below the age of two in an effort to kill the Saviour, JESUS CHRIST.

2.   She taught her son to be evil. *He too walked in the ways of the house of Ahab, for his mother encouraged him in doing wrong. ⁴ He did evil in the eyes of the Lord, as the house of Ahab had done, for after his father's death they became his advisers, to his undoing.* **2 Chronicles 22:3**

Mothers have a significant amount of influence in a child's life and their input has been known to shape the thoughts of a person as they grow. Therefore, a mother like Athaliah not only acted with evil intentions but encouraged her own son to propagate these evil actions as well. In those days we can infer that he murdered, stole, imprisoned, worshiped Baal, was involved in orgies and did nearly everything else imaginable that was evil.

3. **She took over the rule of Judah.** *He remained hidden with them at the temple of God for six years while Athaliah ruled the land.* **2 Chronicles 22:10**

Athaliah ruled by force. She showed no regard for GOD'S order or commands. She stood as the only female to become a king in Judah; she achieved this by murder and evil practice.

Her mind was so corrupt with evil that she even accused Jehoiada, the priest who was doing the right thing by installing Joash to the rulership of the nation, of committing treason! This comes from a woman who was a cold hearted murderer.

4. **She caused unrest for everyone in the nation.** "*...and all the people of the land*

rejoiced. And the city was quiet, because Athaliah had been slain with the sword." **2 Chronicles 23:21** We can tell the kind of state the people were living in at that time; it must have been governed by fear, established by force and delivered by the most corrupt type of people. We should note that Athaliah did not achieve her murderous status by herself; she must have persuaded others to join forces with her. We know this because of Jehoida's statement in **2 Chronicles 23:14**:

Jehoiada the priest sent out the commanders of units of a hundred, who were in charge of the troops, and said to them: "Bring her out between the ranks[b] and put to the sword anyone who follows her.

What can we in the 21st Century learn from Athaliah?

1. **Athaliah is definitely an example of how one's family environment can shape your future.** It is a fact that Athaliah came from an evil family and this biased her towards that direction; but she had a choice. Just because our background was of a particular kind does not mean that must be our future. We have seen people from broken families go on to have successful marriages. Life has to be

about going down a path we choose irrelevant of the previous environment we grew up in.

2. **One of the most alarming aspects of the events surrounding Athaliah's life is the length she went to achieve her ambition.** We need to watch ourselves and never get carried away because of what we want. In fact, our desires must be tempered with helping others and giving back to the community if we are to leave a good legacy.

3. **Walking in the fear of God.** Proverbs 9:10 and Psalm 111:10 say that "The fear of the LORD is the beginning of wisdom."Athaliah had no fear or regard for GOD or His people. Once that fear was absent, she could have taken almost any detestable action. We must always be governed by love for GOD and neighbours to prevent us from going astray and ensure we live a fulfilled life that impacts others in positive ways.

4. **Athaliah lived by the sword and died by the sword.** According to the law of sowing and reaping, Athaliah reaped what she had sown. She was a murderer who was also killed. James the Elder, in his letter in **James 3:12**, says, *My brothers, can a fig tree bear olives, or*

a grapevine bear figs? Neither can a salt spring produce fresh water.

We can derive from this that positive actions will result in positive results in our lives; what you choose to do will bear fruits for you!

5. **Athaliah caused unrest and people were happy when she was removed.** Anyone who is in leadership, either in the home, office, or business must have an attitude that JESUS had. He said in **Mark 10:45,** *"I did not come to be served but to serve and to give my life as a ransom to many."* If we do not live this way, people will rejoice when we are removed and that will be of no joy to us!

6. **Like Athaliah found out the hard way, God's sovereign plan can never be thwarted.** Job said this in **Job 42:2,** *"I know that you can do all things; no plan of yours can be thwarted."* This makes GOD sovereign. Rather than try to go against GOD'S plan, which is a fruitless effort, twenty-first century people should seek to know GOD'S plan and follow it!

Profile

Boomy Tokan is the founder and business tutor of **"Start Your Business in 30 Days" programme.** His experience spans across practical involvement in business and training of more than 1000 Start Up Business owners.

He has set up and run businesses in Property, Music, Management, and Fashion industries. **Many were very successful and others failed miserably.** Through them all he has learnt tremendous lessons that make him a knowledgeable, instructive and experienced teacher!

Whilst at Portobello Business Centre in London (One of the leading Enterprise Centres in Europe), **Boomy Tokan created and delivered Business** Training Programs plus One to One advice to Start Up Advice sessions.

He has also taught "The Business Planning" programme at City University London.

Over the past years **he has helped raise more than £300,000 (nearly $500,000) in small amounts for small businesses.** His experience on writing business plans and his understanding of how to raise finance has been of great benefit for many people.

As a Business Seminar Speaker he continues to contribute to the lives of many people.

Those who attend his courses say: "This facilitator knows what he is about and has a wide field of experience" Charles A

"I realise that I can just get up and do it…." Ros S

"Very insightful and encouraging" Precious O
"Great workshop" Peter D

"This workshop was very helpful" Lillian J and many more!

Boomy believes in giving back to the community and so he runs courses for Newham Business Start Up in London where he helps the underprivileged to access life transforming business information.

He has written over 100 articles for ezine.com and is a author of several books ("How to Write Your First Business Plan: With Outline and Templates Book"; "New Year's Resolutions: The Guide to Getting It Right"; "How to Raise Money for Your Business: The Ultimate Guide For Start Up

Businesses") published on Amazon Kindle that have entered the top 100 of the Entrepreneurship and motivational categories. His books are simply loaded with useful information that is life changing.

His book on **"How To Write Your First Business Plan" has received over Forty Two 5 Star reviews** with comments

like:

" This is really a comprehensive guide to writing a business plan." **Sandra**

" The book reads very easily, and the examples provided allow for a quick understanding of what the author is writing about." **Luke Glasscock**

" It was detailed while still maintaining a comprehensible overview of the structure and what should be taken into account when writing your business plan. " **Michael Matthews**

Have You Got Your FREE "Start Your Own Business In 30 Days" Guide

www.ingramcontent.com/pod-product-compliance
Lightning Source LLC
Chambersburg PA
CBHW051535170526
45165CB00002B/747